Make Money

With

Darvas Box Trading

"Unlocking Profit Potential with Darvas Box Trading"

Copyright : 2024

- BIPLOV SOREN

Disclaimer

The author is not an investment advisor and the information being given in this book is for study purposes only. Information is being presented without consideration of the investment objective, risk tolerance or financial circumstances of any specific investor. You are responsible for your own investment decisions. We urge our readers to seek professional advice before acting on the basis of any information contained in this book.

Acknowledgments

I would like to thank Nicolas Darvas(Darvas Box Theory), JohnMuchow(Darvas Box Theory Indicator) and TradingView(https://in.tradingview.com/) as all the charts which are used in this book are taken from it.

" This book is dedicated to all the stock

market traders in the world "

CONTENTS

Introduction

CHAPTER 1 : Understanding Darvas Box Trading   1

CHAPTER 2 : How to Select Stocks   4

CHAPTER 3 : Darvas Box Trading Setup   12

CHAPTER 4 : Entry and Exit Strategies   16

CHAPTER 5 : Real-life Case Studies in Darvas Box Trading   27

CHAPTER 6 : Risk Management   33

CHAPTER 7 : Common Mistakes to Avoid   40

CHAPTER 8 : Building a Winning Mindset   47

CHAPTER 9 : Psychology of Darvas Box Trading   55

INTRODUCTION:

Welcome to the fascinating world of Darvas Box Trading, a time-tested methodology that has revolutionized the way traders approach the financial markets. In this introduction, we will embark on a journey into the principles, strategies, and potential of Darvas Box Trading, uncovering how it can empower you to navigate the markets with confidence and achieve your trading goals. Darvas Box Trading is named after Nicolas Darvas, a legendary figure who rose to prominence in the 1950s as both a successful dancer and investor. His journey from ballroom floors to trading floors led him to develop a systematic approach to trading that has since become a cornerstone of technical analysis. At its core, Darvas Box Trading is a trend-following strategy that focuses on identifying and riding strong upward or downward trends in the market. The methodology relies on the concept of "boxes," which represent price ranges where significant buying or selling pressure is observed. In this guide, we will explore the key principles of Darvas Box Trading, including how to identify potential breakout candidates, establish entry and exit points, and manage risk effectively. Whether you're a beginner trader or an experienced investor, Darvas Box Trading offers a practical framework for making informed trading decisions and maximizing your profitability in the markets.

Throughout this journey, we will delve into real-world examples, case studies, and practical tips to help you understand the nuances of Darvas Box Trading and apply it to your own trading strategy. By the end of this guide, you will have the knowledge and tools necessary to harness the power of Darvas Box Trading and take your trading to new heights. So, let's dive in and discover the transformative potential of Darvas Box Trading to elevate your trading journey and achieve success in the dynamic world of finance.

CHAPTER 1

Understanding Darvas Box Trading

Darvas Box Trading is a methodology developed by Nicolas Darvas, a dancer-turned-trader who achieved significant success in the stock market in the 1950s and 1960s. Darvas Box Trading is based on the concept of identifying and trading trends using a systematic approach. At the heart of Darvas Box Trading is the idea of "boxes," which represent price ranges where significant buying or selling pressure is observed.

Darvas used a combination of price and volume to identify these boxes, looking for patterns of increasing volume and price movement within a confined range. Once a box is identified, Darvas would enter a trade when the price broke out of the box, indicating a potential trend continuation. He would then set a stop-loss order just below the bottom of the box to manage risk. Darvas Box Trading is a trend-following strategy, meaning that it aims to capitalize on established trends in the market. Traders using this approach 4 typically focus on stocks or other assets with strong upward or downward momentum, as these are more likely to produce profitable trades. One of the key benefits of Darvas Box Trading is its simplicity. The methodology relies on clear rules and criteria for identifying potential trading opportunities, making it accessible to traders of all levels of experience. However, like any trading strategy, Darvas Box Trading also has its limitations and risks. It may not perform as well in choppy or range-bound markets, where price movements are less predictable. Additionally, traders must be disciplined in adhering to their trading plan and managing risk effectively to avoid significant losses. Overall, Darvas Box Trading offers traders a systematic approach to identifying and trading trends in the market. By understanding the principles and techniques behind this methodology, traders can potentially improve their trading performance and achieve their financial goals.

CHAPTER 2

How to Select Stocks

To select stocks hitting 52-week highs from the National Stock Exchange (NSE) of India for Darvas Box Trading, you can follow these steps:

Step-by-Step Process

1. Use NSE Website or Financial Portals

• Visit the NSE website or financial portals like Moneycontrol, Screener, or Investing.com, which provide data on stocks hitting 52-week highs.

2. Screen for 52-Week Highs

• Use the screening tools to filter stocks that are trading at or near their 52-week highs.

3. Additional Screening Criteria

• Apply additional filters based on volume, earnings growth, and other fundamental and technical factors to narrow down the list of potential stocks.

Screening Process on Financial Portals

Using NSE Website:

1. Visit the NSE Website:

• Go to NSE India.

2. Navigate to Market Data:

• Click on "Market Data" and then select "52 Week High/Low" under the "Equity Stock" section.

3. Filter 52-Week Highs:

• Review the list of stocks making 52-week highs.

4. Check Volume and Price Action:

• Note the trading volume and price action of the stocks.

Using Moneycontrol:

1. Visit Moneycontrol:

• Go to Moneycontrol.

2. Navigate to Markets:

- Under the "Markets" tab, select "52 Week High/Low."

3. Filter for 52-Week Highs:

- Choose the filter for stocks hitting 52-week highs.

4. Analyze Stocks:

- Look at the stock details including volume, P/E ratio, earnings growth, etc.

Using Screener.in:

1. Visit Screener:

- Go to Screener.in.

2. Create Custom Filter:

- Use the "Create New Filter" option to set criteria for stocks trading at 52-week highs.

3. Apply Additional Filters:

• Add filters for volume (e.g., average volume > 500,000 shares) and earnings growth (e.g., EPS growth > 15%).

4. Review the List:

• Analyze the filtered list for potential Darvas Box candidates.

Example Screening Criteria Criteria on Screener.in:

• Price near 52-Week High : High / Close < 1.05

• Average Volume : Average volume > 500000

• Earnings Growth : 5 Years EPS growth > 15

• Market Capitalization : Market Cap > 1000 Cr

Example Selection

Assuming the following stocks meet the criteria:

1. Reliance Industries Ltd.

- 52-Week High: INR 2600

- Current Price: INR 2550

- Average Volume: 1,200,000 shares

- EPS Growth (5 Years): 18%

2. Tata Consultancy Services Ltd. (TCS)

- 52-Week High: INR 3600

- Current Price: INR 3550

- Average Volume: 900,000 shares

- EPS Growth (5 Years): 16%

3. HDFC Bank Ltd.

- 52-Week High: INR 1700

- Current Price: INR 1680

- Average Volume: 800,000 shares

- EPS Growth (5 Years): 15%

Implementing Darvas Box Strategy

1. Identify Darvas Box:

- Draw boxes around periods of consolidation and set upper and lower boundaries based on historical highs and lows.

2. Monitor Volume:

• Ensure breakout above the upper boundary occurs with significant volume.

3. Set Stop-Loss:

• Place stop-loss orders slightly below the lower boundary of the box to manage risk.

Conclusion Selecting stocks from the NSE hitting 52-week highs involves using financial portals and screening tools to filter stocks based on specific criteria. By applying additional filters such as volume and earnings growth, you can identify strong candidates for the Darvas Box Trading strategy. Regular monitoring and analysis are essential to successfully implement the strategy.

CHAPTER 3

Darvas Box Trading Setup

The Darvas Box indicator is a technical analysis tool named after NicolasDarvas, a renowned trader who developed the method during the mid-20th century. It aims to identify consolidation phases and potential breakout opportunities in the stock market.

Time Frame – Daily/Weekly

Using Indicator(Tradingview Website) :

1. Darvas Box Theory – Tracking Uptrends(JohnMuchow).

2. Volume (Setting>MA Length 20>Tick Volume MA).

Here's how the Darvas Box indicator works:

1. Box Formation : The indicator creates boxes or rectangles on the price chart, representing price ranges where the stock is consolidating. These boxes are drawn based on specific criteria, typically involving the highest high and lowest low within a defined period (Image 1).

Image 1 — Darvas Box Formation

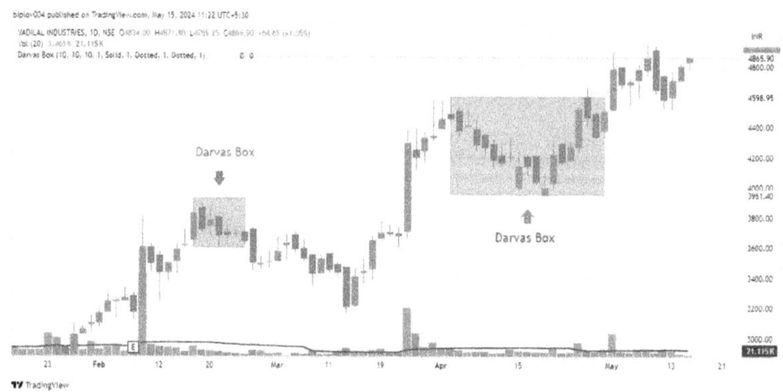

2. Breakout Candle : Traders look for breakouts from the Darvas Boxes, which occur when the stock's price moves above or below the boundaries of the box. A breakout above the upper boundary signals potential bullish momentum, while a breakout below the lower boundary suggests potential bearish momentum (Image 2).

Image 2 — Breakout Candle

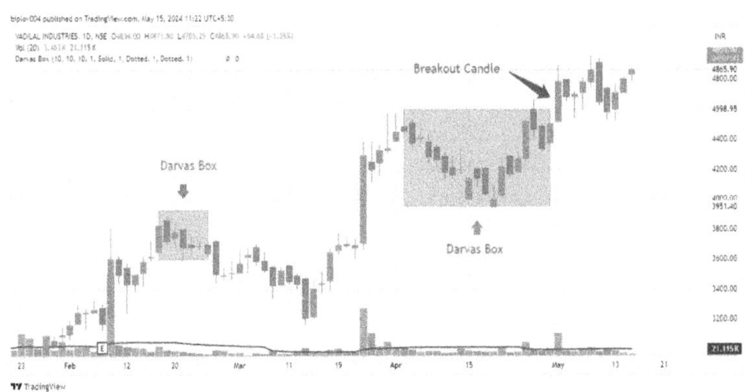

3. Volume Confirmation : Darvas emphasized the importance of volume confirmation when trading breakouts. Traders often look for increasing volume accompanying the breakout, as it validates the strength of the move (Image 3).

Image 3 — Volume Increase

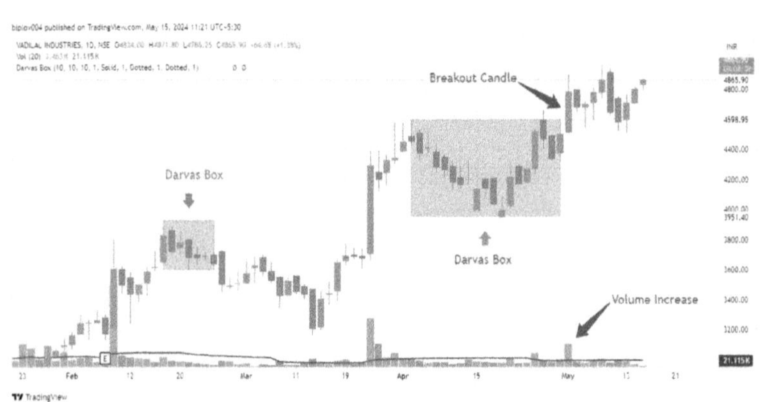

CHAPTER 4

Entry and Exit Strategies

Darvas Box Trading relies on identifying clear entry and exit points based on the formation of "boxes" around periods of price consolidation. Here's how to determine entry and exit points for this strategy:

Identifying the Darvas Box

1. Upper Boundary:

• The upper boundary of the Darvas Box is set at the highest price reached during a period of consolidation.

2. Lower Boundary:

- The lower boundary is the lowest price reached during the same period. (Image 4)

Image 4 (1 Upper Boundary & 2 Lower Boundary)

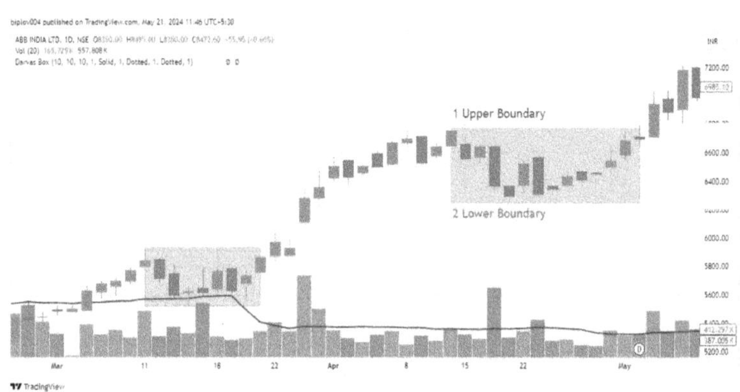

Entry Points

1. Breakout Confirmation:

• Enter a long position when the stock price breaks above the upper boundary of the Darvas Box on higher-than-average volume. This breakout should be confirmed by a significant increase in trading volume, indicating strong buying interest.

2. Buy on Pullback:

• Another entry strategy is to buy on a pullback to the upper boundary after a breakout, ensuring the breakout holds as a new support level.(Image 5)

Image 5 (1 Breakout Confirmation & 2 Buy on Pullback)

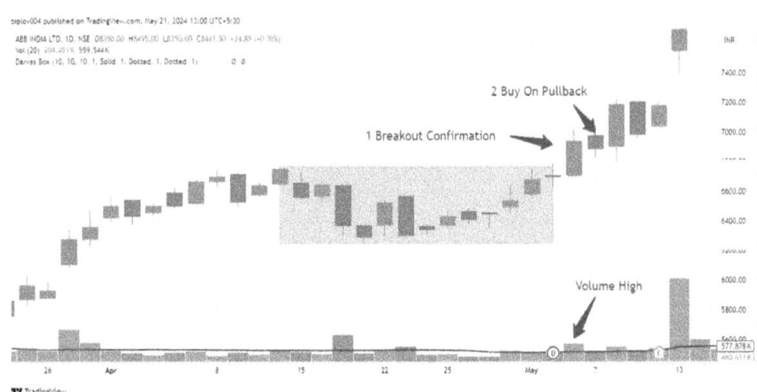

Exit Points

1. Stop-Loss:

• Place a stop-loss slightly below the lower boundary of the Darvas Box to protect against downside risk. This helps limit potential losses if the breakout turns out to be false.

2. Trailing Stop:

• Use a trailing stop to lock in profits as the stock price moves higher. This stop-loss can be adjusted upwards as the stock price rises, typically set at a certain percentage below the current price or below the latest swing low.

3. Price Targets:

• Set price targets based on technical analysis or a predefined risk-reward ratio. You can exit part or all of your position when these targets are reached.(Image 6)

Image 6 (1 Stop-Loss 2 Trailing Stop 3 Price Targets)

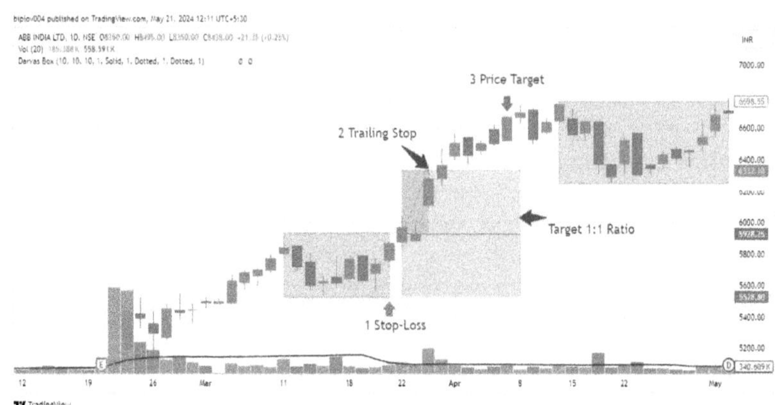

Practical Example

Let's go through a practical example using a hypothetical stock:

Image 7 — Ingersoll Rand Stock

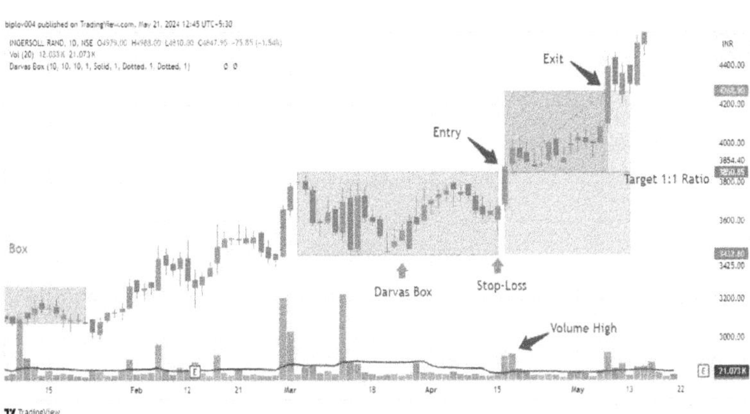

Identifying the Box (Image 7)

- Stock: Ingersoll Rand.

- Upper Boundary: INR 3850.85 (highest price during consolidation)

- Lower Boundary: INR 3432.80 (lowest price during consolidation)

Entry Point

- Breakout: The stock breaks above INR 3850.85 with high volume.

- Entry: Buy at INR 3875 after confirming the breakout with volume.

Exit Points

- Stop-Loss: Set at INR 3430 (slightly below the lower boundary).

• Trailing Stop: Adjust to 5% below the highest price reached after breakout.

• Price Target: Based on technical analysis, set a target at INR 4268 .

Detailed Steps

1. Formation of Darvas Box:

• Observe the stock consolidating between INR 3850.85 and INR 3432.80 for a period (e.g., 2-3 weeks).

2. Breakout and Entry:

• Stock breaks above INR 3850.85.

• Confirm the breakout with increased volume (e.g., volume doubles the average).

- Enter a position at INR 3875.

3. Stop-Loss Placement:

- Set a stop-loss at INR 3430 to limit downside risk.

4. Trailing Stop:

- As the stock moves up, adjust the trailing stop to maintain a 5% buffer below the highest price. For instance, if the stock reaches INR 4268, the trailing stop would be at INR 4054.

5. Exiting the Position:

- If the stock hits the target price of INR 4268, consider selling part or all of the positions.

- Alternatively, if the stock drops to the trailing stop level, exit to secure profits.

Monitoring and Adjustments

- **Regular Monitoring:**

- Continuously monitor the stock's price action and volume.

- Adjust stop-loss and trailing stop levels as necessary to protect gains.

- **Review Market Conditions:**

- Consider broader market trends and news that might affect the stock's By following these steps, you can effectively implement the Darvas Box Trading strategy to identify optimal entry and exit points, thus maximizing potential profits while managing risks.

CHAPTER 5

Real-life Case Studies in Darvas Box Trading

Image 8 – Manorama Industries Ltd

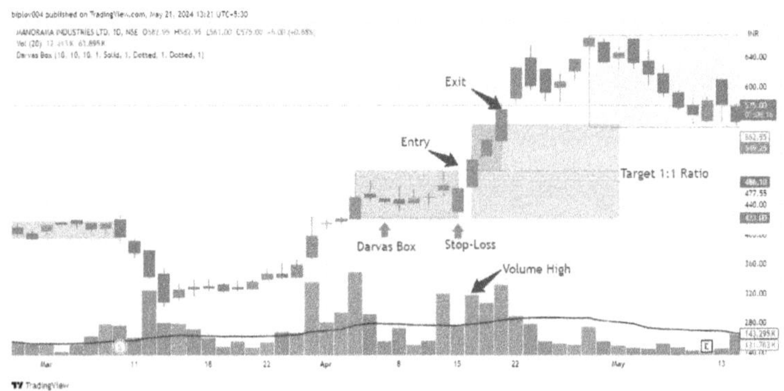

Stock Name - Manorama Industries Ltd (Image 8)

Entry Date - 16 April 2024

Entry Price - INR 491

Exit Price – INR 550

Target – 1:1 Ratio

Stop-Loss – INR 422

Image – 9 Trent Ltd

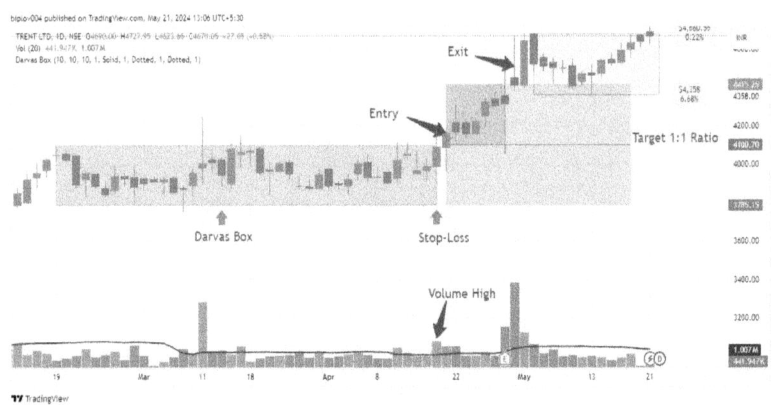

Stock Name - Trent Ltd (Image 9)

Entry Date - 19 April 2024

Entry Price - INR 4158

Exit Price – INR 4449

Target – 1:1 Ratio

Stop-Loss – INR 3785

Image – 10 Century Textiles & Industries Ltd

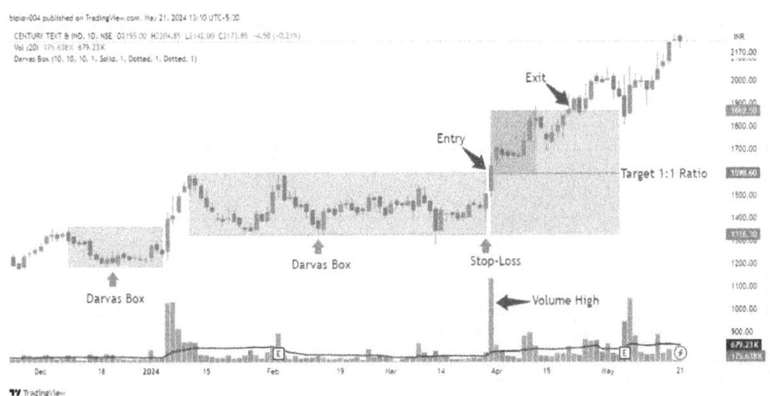

Stock Name - Century Textiles & Industries Ltd (Image 10)

Entry Date - 28 March 2024

Entry Price - INR 1627

Exit Price – INR 1892

Target – 1:1 Ratio

StopLoss – INR 1326

Image – 11 Mazagon Dock Shipbuilders Ltd

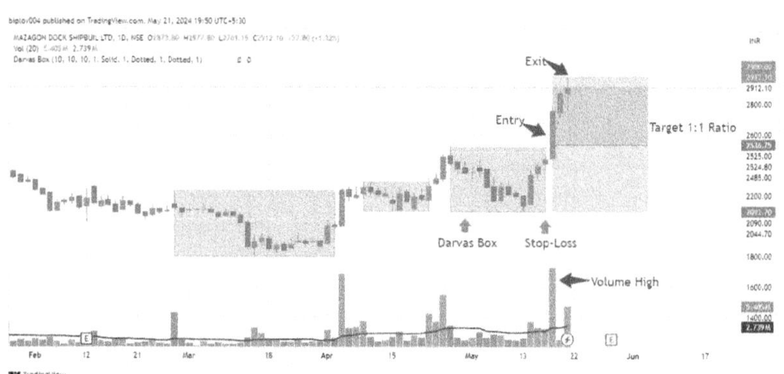

Stock Name - Mazagon Dock Shipbuilders Ltd (Image 11)

Entry Date - 17 May 2024

Entry Price - INR 2252

Exit Price - INR 2977

Target – 1:1 Ratio

StopLoss – INR 2029

Image – 12 Bharat Bijlee Ltd

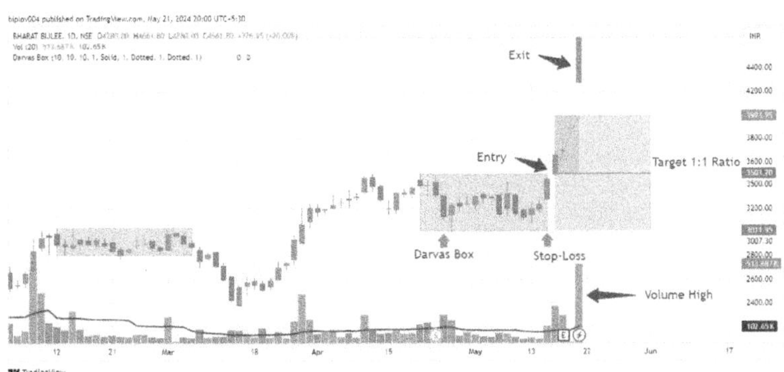

Stock Name - Bharat Bijlee Ltd (Image 12)

Entry Date - 16 May 2024

Entry Price - INR 3510

Exit Price – INR 4627

Target – 1:1 Ratio

StopLoss – INR 3011

CHAPTER 6

Risk Management

In the context of Darvas Box trading, a risk management strategy is crucial for managing potential losses and optimizing returns. Darvas Box trading is a technical analysis method developed by Nicolas Darvas, which involves identifying and trading stocks that break out of a predefined price range or "box". Effective risk management in Darvas Box trading involves several key components:

A. Key Components of Risk Management in Darvas Box Trading

B. Position Sizing:

a. Objective: Determine the appropriate amount of capital to allocate to each trade to manage risk effectively.

b. Methods: Use a fixed percentage of total capital for each trade, such as 1-2%. This prevents overexposure to any single trade.

C. Setting Stop-Loss Orders:

a. Objective: Limit potential losses on each trade by automatically selling a stock if its price falls to a predetermined level.

b. Methods: Place stop-loss orders slightly below the lower boundary of the Darvas Box. This ensures that if the price moves against the position, the loss is minimized.

D. Trailing Stops:

a. Objective: Protect profits while allowing for potential gains.

b. Methods: Adjust the stop-loss level upward as the stock price rises, maintaining a fixed distance below the current price. This distance can be based on a percentage or a fixed amount.

E. Diversification:

a. Objective: Spread risk across multiple trades and asset classes to reduce the impact of any single losing trade.

b. Methods: Avoid concentrating too much capital in one stock or sector. Trade in a variety of stocks from different industries.

F. Entry and Exit Rules:

a. Objective: Define clear criteria for entering and exiting trades based on the Darvas Box methodology.

b. Methods: Enter a trade when the stock price breaks above the upper boundary of the Darvas Box with high volume. Exit a trade if the price falls below the lower boundary or hits the stop-loss level.

G. Risk-Reward Ratio:

a. Objective: Ensure that the potential reward from a trade justifies the risk taken.

b. Methods: Aim for a minimum risk-reward ratio, such as 1:2 or higher. This means the potential profit should be at least twice the potential loss.

H. Regular Review and Adjustment:

a. Objective: Continuously monitor trades and the overall market conditions to make necessary adjustments.

b. Methods: Review performance periodically, adjust stop-loss levels, and reassess position sizes based on changing market conditions and portfolio performance.

c. Practical Example of Risk Management in Darvas Box Trading

I. Identifying the Box: Suppose a trader identifies a Darvas Box for Stock A with an upper boundary at $100 and a lower boundary at $90.

J. Position Sizing: With a total capital of $10,000 and a risk policy of 2% per trade, the trader decides to risk $200 per trade.

K. Stop-Loss Order: The trader sets a stop-loss order at $89 (slightly below the lower boundary of the box) to limit the loss if the trade goes against them.

L. Entering the Trade: The trader enters a position when the stock price breaks above $100 with significant volume.

M. Trailing Stop: As the stock price increases, the trader adjusts the stop-loss order upward, maintaining a distance that locks in profits while allowing for potential price increases.

N. Risk-Reward Ratio: The trader targets a price of $120 for a 2:1 risk-reward ratio, meaning they are willing to risk $10 per share for a potential gain of $20 per share.

O. Review and Adjustment: The trader regularly reviews the trade's progress and overall portfolio, making adjustments to stop-loss levels and position sizes as needed.

P. By incorporating these risk management strategies, traders using the Darvas Box method can better manage potential losses, protect profits, and increase their chances of long-term trading success.

CHAPTER 7

Common Mistakes to Avoid in Darvas Box Trading

Darvas Box trading can be a powerful method when used correctly, but traders often make common mistakes that can undermine their success. Here are some common mistakes to avoid in Darvas Box trading:

1. Ignoring Volume:

- **Mistake:** Entering trades without considering the volume.

• **Correction:** Ensure that breakouts are accompanied by significant volume, as this indicates stronger market interest and potential for a sustained move.

2. Setting Inappropriate Box Boundaries:

• **Mistake:** Misidentifying the upper and lower boundaries of the Darvas Box.

• **Correction:** Carefully analyze historical price action to correctly identify the high and low points that define the box. Avoid using too short or too long time frames.

3. Overtrading:

• **Mistake:** Taking too many trades simultaneously or trading too frequently.

• **Correction:** Be selective with trades, only entering when the criteria are clearly met. Overtrading can lead to excessive transaction costs and increased risk.

4. Poor Risk Management:

• **Mistake:** Failing to set stop-loss orders or using improper position sizes.

• **Correction:** Always set stop-loss orders slightly below the lower boundary of the box and use appropriate position sizing to manage risk.

5. Chasing Breakouts:

• **Mistake:** Entering trades after the initial breakout move, often due to fear of missing out (FOMO).

- **Correction:** Stick to your trading plan and enter positions as soon as the breakout occurs with confirming volume. Avoid entering late and at higher prices.

6. Ignoring Market Conditions:

- **Mistake:** Trading without considering overall market trends and conditions.

- **Correction:** Take into account broader market trends and avoid trading against the overall market direction. Darvas Box trading works best in trending markets.

7. Failure to Adjust Stop-Loss Orders:

- **Mistake:** Not adjusting stop-loss orders as the price moves in your favor.

● **Correction:** Use trailing stops to lock in profits while allowing for further gains. Adjust stop-loss orders upward as the stock price increases.

8. Emotional Trading:

● **Mistake:** Letting emotions drive trading decisions, such as holding onto losing positions out of hope or fear.

● **Correction:** Follow your trading plan and predefined rules strictly. Avoid making decisions based on emotions.

9. Inadequate Research:

● **Mistake:** Entering trades without sufficient research or understanding of the stock and its fundamentals.

● **Correction:** Conduct thorough research on the stocks you are trading, including fundamental analysis and understanding the company's business model.

10.Ignoring Exit Strategies:

• **Mistake:** Focusing solely on entry points and neglecting exit strategies.

• **Correction:** Define clear exit strategies, including profit targets and stop-loss levels, before entering trades. Stick to these strategies to avoid impulsive decisions.

11. Lack of Patience:

• **Mistake:** Not giving trades enough time to develop within the Darvas Box framework.

• **Correction:** Be patient and allow trades to play out according to your plan. Avoid premature exits unless there is a clear signal to do so.

Conclusion

By being aware of these common mistakes and taking steps to avoid them, traders can improve their success rate with Darvas Box trading. Consistent application of sound risk management principles, careful analysis, and disciplined execution are key to achieving favorable outcomes in this trading strategy.

CHAPTER 8

Building a Winning Mindset

Building a winning mindset for Darvas Box trading is crucial for consistent success. Here are key elements and strategies to develop a mindset conducive to thriving in this trading approach:

Key Elements of a Winning Mindset

1. Discipline:

- **Stick to Your Plan:** Adhere strictly to your trading plan, including entry and exit points, stop-loss levels, and position sizing.

- **Avoid Impulsiveness:** Resist the urge to make spontaneous decisions based on short-term market movements or emotions.

2. Patience:

- **Wait for Clear Signals:** Only enter trades when all your criteria are met, such as price breaking out of the Darvas Box with high volume.

- **Allow Trades to Develop:** Give your trades enough time to reach their potential, avoiding premature exits unless warranted by your strategy.

3. Confidence:

• **Trust Your Analysis:** Believe in your trading system and the analysis that led to your decisions. Confidence helps you stay calm under pressure.

• **Learn Continuously:** Constantly improve your knowledge and skills to build confidence in your trading abilities.

4. Resilience:

• **Handle Losses Constructively:** Accept that losses are part of trading and use them as learning opportunities rather than letting them affect your confidence.

• **Maintain Emotional Balance:** Keep emotions in check, whether facing gains or losses, to make rational decisions.

5. Adaptability:

• **Adjust to Market Conditions:** Be ready to adapt your strategies based on changing market conditions while staying true to your core principles.

• **Continuous Improvement:** Regularly review and refine your trading strategies and mindset to stay effective.

Strategies to Develop a Winning Mindset

1. Set Realistic Goals:

• Define clear, achievable objectives for your trading activities. Focus on steady growth rather than quick profits.

2. Develop a Robust Trading Plan:

• Include detailed criteria for trade entries, exits, stop-loss levels, and risk management. Review and adjust the plan periodically.

3. Practice Consistent Risk Management:

• Never risk more than a small percentage of your capital on a single trade. Use stop-loss orders to limit potential losses.

4. Keep a Trading Journal:

• Document all trades, including the rationale behind them, outcomes, and any lessons learned. Reviewing this journal can provide valuable insights into your trading behavior and help you improve.

5. Focus on the Process, Not the Profits:

• Emphasize executing your strategy correctly rather than obsessing over the financial outcomes. Good processes lead to good results over time.

6. Stay Educated:

• Continuously learn about market trends, trading strategies, and new developments in technical analysis. Knowledge enhances your confidence and decision-making abilities.

7. Maintain a Healthy Lifestyle:

• Ensure physical and mental well-being by getting enough sleep, eating healthily, and exercising regularly. A healthy body supports a sharp mind.

8. Surround Yourself with Positive Influences:

• Engage with a community of traders who share your mindset and can offer support, advice, and encouragement. Avoid negative influences that can undermine your confidence and focus.

Practical Steps to Implement These Strategies

1. Morning Routine: Start your day with a routine that includes reviewing market news, your trading plan, and visualizing successful trades.

2. Mindfulness and Meditation: Practice mindfulness or meditation to stay centered and reduce stress, enhancing your ability to make clear-headed decisions.

3. Regular Breaks: Take regular breaks during trading sessions to avoid fatigue and maintain focus.

4. Review Sessions: At the end of each trading day, review your trades, journal entries, and reflect on what went well and what could be improved.

By developing and maintaining a winning mindset through these elements and strategies, you can enhance your discipline, patience, confidence, resilience, and adaptability, all of which are crucial for success in Darvas Box trading.

CHAPTER 9

Psychology of Darvas Box Trading

Importance of Trading Psychology

Trading psychology plays a crucial role in the success of any trading strategy, including the Darvas Box method. Understanding and managing your emotions, maintaining discipline, and developing a resilient mindset can significantly impact your trading outcomes. Key psychological aspects include:

1. Emotional Control: Being able to manage fear and greed is essential. Fear can prevent you from entering trades or cause you to exit prematurely, while greed can lead to over-trading or holding onto positions for too long.

2. Discipline: Sticking to your trading plan and rules, even in the face of market volatility or emotional impulses, is vital for consistent success.

3. Patience: Waiting for the right setups and not forcing trades is a hallmark of successful traders. The Darvas Box method relies on specific conditions being met before entering a trade.

4. Resilience: The ability to bounce back from losses and not let them affect your future trading decisions is important. Losses are a natural part of trading and must be managed properly.

Common Psychological Pitfalls

1. Overtrading: Entering too many trades without proper analysis can lead to losses. It's important to be selective and patient.

2. Chasing the Market: Trying to enter trades out of FOMO (fear of missing out) can lead to poor decision-making and significant losses.

3. Impulsiveness: Making trades based on gut feelings or external noise rather than your trading strategy.

4. Confirmation Bias: Only seeking out information that confirms your existing beliefs and ignoring data that contradicts them.

Developing a Trading Mindset

1. Create a Routine: Establish a daily trading routine that includes market analysis, reviewing your trading plan, and preparing for potential setups.

2. Use a Trading Journal: Keeping a detailed record of your trades, including the rationale behind them, the outcome, and your emotional state, can help you identify patterns and areas for improvement.

3. Set Realistic Goals: Having clear, achievable goals can keep you focused and motivated. Avoid setting goals based solely on profit and instead focus on process-oriented goals, like following your trading plan.

4. Continuous Learning: Stay updated with market trends, new strategies, and trading psychology. The market is constantly evolving, and so should your knowledge and skills.

Maintaining Discipline

1. Follow Your Plan: Once you've developed your Darvas Box trading plan, stick to it. Avoid making spontaneous decisions that deviate from your strategy.

2. Risk Management: Implement strict risk management rules, such as setting stop-loss orders and position sizing, to protect your capital.

3. Regular Reviews: Periodically review your trading performance and strategy effectiveness. This helps in identifying any deviations and making necessary adjustments.

Emotional Control Techniques

1. Mindfulness and Meditation: Practices that promote mindfulness can help you stay calm and focused, reducing the impact of emotional reactions.

2. Breaks and Downtime: Taking regular breaks from trading can help prevent burnout and keep your mind fresh.

3. Positive Reinforcement: Reward yourself for following your trading rules and plans, regardless of the trade outcomes. This reinforces good habits.

Learning from Mistakes

1. Accept Losses as Part of Trading: Understand that not all trades will be winners. Learning to accept and manage losses is key to long-term success.

2. Analyze Your Mistakes: After a losing trade, analyze what went wrong and how you can avoid similar mistakes in the future. This can be an invaluable learning tool.

3. Stay Objective: Try to remain objective and avoid letting emotions drive your trading decisions. Focus on the data and your strategy.

By addressing these psychological aspects and incorporating them into your trading routine, you can enhance your ability to trade using the Darvas Box method effectively and consistently. Remember, successful trading is as much about mindset and psychology as it is about strategy and analysis.

CHAPTER 10

Checklist for Darvas Box Trades

Pre-Trade Preparation

1. Identify Potential Stocks

○ Use a stock screener to find stocks with strong upward momentum.

○ Ensure the stock meets the criteria for volume and price action.

○ Check for recent news or events that might impact the stock's performance.

2. Fundamental Analysis

o Review the company's financial health.

o Look at key metrics such as earnings growth, revenue trends, and profit margins.

o Ensure the company has a solid business model and growth prospects.

Creating the Darvas Box

1. Determine Upper and Lower Box Limits

o Identify the highest price (resistance level) the stock has reached recently.

o Identify the lowest price (support level) where the stock has shown support.

○ Ensure these levels form a well-defined box with clear boundaries.

2. Volume Confirmation

○ Check that the stock's volume increases when the price approaches the upper limit.

○ Look for decreasing volume during price pullbacks to the lower limit.

Entry Criteria

1. Set Entry Point

○ Plan to enter the trade when the stock price breaks above the upper limit of the Darvas Box.

o Ensure the breakout is confirmed by a significant increase in volume.

2. Set Stop-Loss Order

o Place a stop-loss order just below the lower limit of the Darvas Box to minimize potential losses.

o Adjust the stop-loss order as the stock price moves in your favor (trailing stop).

Managing the Trade

1. Monitor the Trade

o Regularly check the stock's price action and volume.

o Be alert for signs of weakening momentum or potential reversal patterns.

2. Adjust Stop-Loss and Profit Targets

○ As the stock price rises, adjust your stop-loss order to lock in profits.

○ Consider setting a profit target based on technical analysis or a predefined risk-reward ratio.

Exit Criteria

1. Exit the Trade

○ Exit the trade if the stock price falls below the lower limit of the Darvas Box or hits your stop-loss.

○ Take profits if the stock reaches your predefined profit target.

○ Consider exiting if there are significant changes in market conditions or company fundamentals.

Post-Trade Analysis

1. Review and Analyze the Trade

○ Record the details of the trade, including entry and exit points, reasons for the trade, and the outcome.

○ Analyze what worked well and what could be improved.

○ Learn from any mistakes to refine your strategy for future trades.

Psychological and Routine Checks

1. Maintain Discipline

○ Stick to your trading plan and avoid making impulsive decisions.

○ Ensure you are not overtrading and are following your predefined rules.

2. Emotional Control

○ Stay calm and focused during trades, regardless of market movements.

○ Practice mindfulness or stress-relief techniques if needed.

Example Checklist Template

Pre-Trade Preparation

- Screen for potential stocks

- Perform fundamental analysis

Creating the Darvas Box

- Determine upper box limit (resistance)

- Determine lower box limit (support)

- Confirm volume patterns

Entry Criteria

- Set entry point above the upper limit

- Place stop-loss order below the lower limit

Managing the Trade

- Monitor price action and volume

- Adjust stop-loss and set profit targets

Exit Criteria

- Exit at stop-loss or lower box limit breach

- Exit at profit target

- Exit on significant market or company changes

Post-Trade Analysis

- Record trade details

- Analyze trade performance

- Identify lessons learned

Psychological and Routine Checks

- Maintain trading discipline

- Control emotions and stay focused

Using this checklist, traders can systematically apply the Darvas Box method, ensuring consistency and discipline in their trading approach.